MANUAL OF THE SIKKIM-BHUTIA LANGUAGE OR DE-JONG KE

MANUAL

OF

THE SIKKIM-BHUTIA LANGUAGE

OR

DE-JONG KE

By

GRAHAM SANDBERG

GYAN

ISBN : 978-81-212-1680-7(HB)

First Published, 1888

Published, 2018

Published by

Gyan Publishing House
5, Ansari Road
Daryaganj, New Delhi-110002
Phone: 011-47034999, 9811692060
www.gyanbooks.com
E-mail: books@gyanbooks.com

Printed at: G. Print Process, Delhi.

TO THE READER.

The writer of these pages has often wondered why those who spend so many months yearly at Darjiling never seem to take the slightest interest in the language spoken by the bulk of the population there. They may not be aware that the uncouth-sounding chatter of the Bhutias about the place is in reality a dialect of one of the great literary languages of Asia. It differs in many particulars from Tibetan but on examination will be found full of interest, and by no means so barbarous a speech as is supposed. To acquire the Sikkim dialect might form a preliminary step to the study of the Tibetan tongue, which has been so long and strangely neglected. Moreover, now that Sikkim is being fast opened out, the traveller, and especially the missionary, the sportsman and the soldier, will find a knowledge of this dialect most desirable. At any rate an exposition of this Bhutia speech, never previously analysed, is here made for the first time and presented to the public.

Jhansi: N.W.P., July 1888.

INTRODUCTORY NOTE.

The native state of Sikkim is that portion of the Eastern Himalaya Mountains which lies wedged in between the kingdom of Nepal and the independent territory of Bhutan. The northernmost point on the Tibetan frontier falls under Lat. 28° 7' 30" N. and the southern apex lies in Lat. 27° 5' N., barely ten miles north of Darjiling. Comprising as it does some of the highest and most rugged mountains in the world, as well as being rent and parcelled out in every direction by ravines and river-gorges of stupendous depth and labyrinthine course, the actual area of Sikkim cannot with certainty be estimated. However the theoretical superficies measured in one plane may be put down at 2684 square miles and *not* 1550 square miles as given in *Hunter's Gazeteer.* Moreover, before the Darjiling and Kalimpong districts were severed from this little state, the area approached 4000 square miles.

"Sikkim" is only the Gurkha name of the territory we are dealing with. The Tibetan appellation is Dái-jong or "fruit district;" whilst the Lepchas or *Rong-pa* (*i.e.*, "Ravine folk,") said to be the oldest occupants of the country, formerly styled it *Nelyáng* but now call it *Ren-jong.*

In estimating the inhabitants of the country we shall naturally class with them the native population of Darjiling and Kalimpong, who, but for the recent overflux of Nepalese immigrants, are practically one with the Sikkim folk. Tribes of various races have settled in these mountainous regions; but the Dé-jong-pa or Sikkim Bhutias everywhere predominate; and these latter are being constantly augmented by accessions from their Tibetan and Bhutanese cousins. The rightful occupants of the country are apparently the Lepchas whose kings formerly were rulers here. But the Sikkim Bhutias can now fairly claim an historical connection with the land; and, though of Tibetan origin, by this time have acquired an autonomy and local characteristics of their own. This Tibetan race began to over-run Dé-jong or Sikkim some 380 years ago; and the first Bhutia King, P'unts'o Namgyai by name, assumed control here about the same year that King Henry VIIIth ascended the British Throne. These Bhutias came from the province of Tsang in Tibet and doubtless brought with them the then prevailing dialect of that province. Both their sovereigns and their speech have continued to the present day. Although the Lepchas also have maintained their own language: yet, as the Bhutias both in numbers and in power are the predominant people of the land, we may, we think, not unreasonably speak of the Bhutia tongue as the Dé-jong Ké or vernacular of Sikkim. The language in question is admittedly a Tibetan dialect—some doubtless would style it a corrupt Tibetan, because both in vocabulary and grammatical forms it differs from the speech of Lhasa. So far as pronunciation goes, however, it seems to be the speech of Lhasa which has acquired corruptions; whilst the Dē-jong Kè, in common with the dialect of Balti beyond Ladák, has retained, in some notable instances, a purer method of pronunciation—at least a method more in accord with the ancient spelling.

It must not be supposed that the Dé-jong dialect is the general speech of all Tibetans in Sikkim. Our tenancy of Darjiling has attracted many from the mother country and elsewhere, who rarely use, though they may understand, the grammatical peculiarities of the Sikkim folk. In the Kalimpong district many families speak the Tibetan dialect of Bhutan. At Ghum are settled pure Tibetans and Wallung-pa from Nepal, who rather despise the Sikkim race. The Sharpa Bhutias, a cross race between the Lepchas and Bhutias, make use of the Dé-jong vernacular.

The great divergence between the orthography and the pronunciation of Tibetan words is well known. Thus the word spelt *dbugs* ("breath") is sounded as "ū" merely; another spelt *spyod* is pronounced *chö*; but all according to settled rules of orthoëpy. The salutation in Tibetan letters painted up over the entrance to the Bhutia School at Darjiling is written *byon-ba legs-so* (welcome) but is spoken *chönwa le-so.* Naturally the Sikkim Bhutias make use of Tibetan characters and modes of spelling; and those who do write generally eschew the more peculiar colloquialisms of this dialect. As the present treatise is intended to deal with, rather than to avoid, these peculiarities, we shall have no occasion to introduce any but Roman characters into these pages. As a dialect distinct from the general Tibetan language, the Dé-jong Ké cannot claim to be called a written speech. Sikkim indeed in past years has been the native home of literary authors, both of the Lepcha and Bhutia race, who have issued works in their own respective languages. The heads of the two great Sikkim monasteries, Labrong and Tashiding, are always held to be incarnate lamas, having within them the spirits of two of the Buddhist apostles who converted the Lepchas (in part) and the Murmis to the latter faith. Two or three of the line of these incarnate ones have produced in their day religious works, written of course in classical Tibetan. These were printed either at Nart'ang in Tibet or else in Khams. One popular Bhutia composition is said to be indigenous to Sikkim, where it is met with chiefly in MS. form, namely, the *Bkrashis Gsung.* There also exists a Lepcha translation of the book.

The official language of Déjong is Tibetan and in the Kalimpong and Darjiling districts our Government notices are printed collaterally in Bengali and Tibetan. At the Kutcheri in Darjiling the notice boards are covered with lengthy notifications in Tibetan characters and in the Tibetan tongue with the Sikkim style eliminated to the best of the ability of the Bhutia clerks who compose the same However, we have no desire to elevate the Dé-jong Ké to the dignity of a literary language: for it owes all that is literary about it to the mother speech as cultivated at Lhasa, Tashi-lhumpo, and Nart'ang.

The running hand employed in letters and business contracts, as written by the Lamas of Sikkim, appears to be rather different from that in general use in Tibet. We wish we could have reproduced a specimen as written for us by Lama Ugyen Gya ts'o; but the expense of lithography must not be incurred, at least in the present form of this little book.

GRAMMAR

OF THE

DE-JONG LANGUAGE.

The sounds occurring in the Dé-jong dialect of Tibetan are these :—

CONSONANTS.

k ; pronounced as the English k in "king."

kh ; the aspirated k as in the Hindustani "khana."

g ; as our hard g in "goat ;" a letter rarely occurring

ng ; occurring both as an initial and as a final ; at the commencement of a word sounded something as our gn in "gnarled" but more nasal.

ch ; as in our "church."

chh ; the aspirated ch—as the ch and h taken together in sounding the words "reach-hither."

j ; as in our "jim," but generally more aspirated.

ny ; an initial whose sound may be learnt by pronouncing n and y together in such a word as "nyim."

t ; as our t.

d ; as in "den"

th ; not as our "th" but as t and h together in such a combination as "hit him" and as in the Hindi : "thana." We shall represent this sound by *t'*.

dh ; d aspirated as the last letter, to be represented by *d'*.

*_** The four last-named letters sometimes occur with a slightly different sound. Instead of being pronounced with the tongue touching the teeth or gums, they are varied by being sounded with the tongue put back and pressed against the front part of the roof of the mouth. They are then called *cerebrals* ; and will be represented by the ordinary letters with a dot underneath.

p ; as in our "put."

ph ; the last letter aspirated ; not sounded as f, but as the p and h together in "top-heavy ;" here to stand as *p'*.

b ; as the English b.

m ; as in "mast."

ts ; as in "tsi."

ts'h ; same aspirated.

dz; our d and z sounded together as a rough z.
w; as our w in "woof."
zh; as the French j in "jules"—a rough sh.

z;
y;
r;
l;
sh;
s;
h; } all as the English letters.

ky;
gy;
phy; } The k, g, and aspirated p, sounded with y immediately following; the last to be represented here by p'y.

hl; the l aspirated. Not unlike the sound of the Welsh double l.

VOWELS AND DIPHTHONGS.

á; as a in "father."
a; as u in "fun."
e; as a in "lane."
i; as ee in "teem."
ĭ; as i in "tin."
o; always as o in "stone;" never as o in "pot," &c., except in *potso* a boy and about two other words.
u; as oo in "Poona;" shorter than our oo in "pool."
ai; as i in "mine."
au; as au in "taught" or as ou in "ought."
eu; as u in "cue."
ái; the Tibetan mode of sounding their *as*; either like "é" as above, or more correctly as "á" followed rapidly by a very short i (ee). Thus *Dài-jong* or *Dé-jong*.

ö; is our o and e conjoined and sounded with the opening of the mouth narrowed as if about to whistle; or one might describe it as an e said with affectation. In German a well-known sound.

ü; as eu in the French word "feu," pronounced with the lips pointed and almost closed.

At first when speaking it will be found difficult to give the sounds the exact accent, or rather twang, of the Bhutia natives. The two last mentioned diphthongs are puzzling sounds to imitate; and yet, if an ordinary o and u were to be used in their places, perfectly different words would be understood to those you intended.

"Ng," though easy enough to say as a final, when occurring as the *first* letter of a word requires much practice to acquire. Two separate sounds must not be made of the n and g. It is one letter, and therefore a single nasal "a" sound, uttered with the roof of the mouth, must alone be heard. Practice "unga" and that will lead you to the correct sound.

To say "gy" rightly, personally I have found it almost advisable, strange though it may seem, to pronounce it as dy. Thus *gyuk-she* "to run" is almost *dyuk-she.*

Remember u is always long as our oo; not as our u in "duck," but nearly as our u in "put."

In two-letter syllables ending in o, as *bo*, *mo*, the o is heard rather as an abrupt u (oo) yet still an o sound.

Now and then in these pages we have employed accents to shew where the stress should be laid; but á merely indicates the long Irish "a" as given above.

I.—THE ARTICLE.

The indefinite article a, an, is represented by *chik* placed after the noun or adjective. The final k is generally, however, left unsounded: *Pum chi'* a girl.

We do not often use this article except when the noun is in the nominative case, unless indeed it occurs in the sense of "one." Thus "a boy" will be *Potso chi;* "of a boy" *Potso kyi;* "of one boy" *Potso chi yi.*

The definite article is very much in use: *di* the. It is heard with inflected nouns as well as when the latter stand in the nominative. When the noun has a possessive pronoun attached we often find *di* still added (see IV. I. *b*)

Ordinarily *di* follows its noun; but where any singling out of the noun is desired we have one *di* placed before and another *di* after the word, *e.g.*, *di p'ya di* the bird. (see also IV. 3. Exam.)

II.—NOUN SUBSTANTIVES.

1.—In the Dé-jong Ké the different cases of the noun are specified by means of short syllables, called postpositions, annexed to the words:—

Khim chi a house.

Nom: *Khim chi*	a house.
Gen: *Khim kyi*	of a house.
Dat: *Khim lo*	to a house.
Accus: *Khim* or *Khim lo*	a house.
Loc: *Khim na*	at or in a house.
Abl: *Khim ne* or *le*	from a house.
Agentive: (wanting)	

Jágma chi a squirrel.

Nom : *Jágma chi*	a squirrel.
Gen : *Jágma-i* or *yi*	of a squirrel.
Dat : *Jágma lo*	to a squirrel.
Accus : *Jágma* or *Jagma lo*	a squirrel.
Loc : *Jágma na*	in a squirrel.
Abl : *Jágma ne* or *le*	from a squirrel.
Agent : *Jágma yī*	by a squirrel.

After a final vowel the gen. affix ought to be "i" or "yi" sounded separately; but *kyi* is often employed, especially after the article: e. g., *di-kyi* of the.

The plural number is not often expressed; but where doubt would arise, the particles *chá* or *ts'o* may be added, *e. g., nyi-lam* a dream *nyi-lam chá* dreams; *Gyá-mi* a Chinaman *Gyá-mi ts'o* Chinamen, Chinese. The case signs would follow the plural particle.

Where any case other than the nominative occurs the definite article is not expressed, e. g.

Potso-kyi lu di: The song of the boy; the boy's song.

Khyi-da di álü lo so-tap ong: The dog will bite the cat.

In the latter sentence *álü lo* is the accus. after the verb *so-tap ong* will bite, *so-tap* meaning *tap* strike, *so* (with the) teeth.

However the definite article is sometimes used with the accus. when the verb is in the Imperative Mood :—

Gom di p'i: Open the door! *To-za di tso:* cook the food!

The other connections of nouns such as "with," "upon," "under," "unto," will be explained under the heading Post-positions. These are indeed at times added where we should not consider their introduction required, as where we should use only a simple case sign, *e. g.*

Shing audi teng-khá dzek: Climb this tree.

Here *teng khá* "upon" is introduced in accordance with Tibetan idiom; and placed after *Shing audi* "this tree." The accus. case may be expressed by the simple word without the affix *lo* where no ambiguity would result as to which were the nominative, especially in imperative sentences, as in the example given above :—

Gom di p'i: Open the door.

But where a dative sense is implied in any way the *lo* must be used :—

Mi-lo lam di ten nang: Shew (to) the man the way.

2.—A rather important case rule to be remembered is however this :—

Where both subject and object occur in any sentence, the subject is put in the agentive case, except where the verb of the sentence is part of the verb "to be."

Rule though this is, it is generally not observed by the uneducated; and therefore we shall not keep to it in our conversational examples to be given hereafter; the nominative being usually heard as in English. One Example is now given :—

Bágrak kyī ts'áng p'yá chen du': A spider is making a web.

We conclude the present section by appending a classified list of useful nouns :—

Animate Beings.

mi man
pumo woman
gárok husband
kyermen wife
áp'á father
ámu mother
p'ugu child
potso boy
pum girl
shempa youth
pumo daughter
áp'i grandmother
pu son
pün brothers
á-cho eldest brother
nu-wo younger brother
singmo sister
tá horse
te mule
ká-shá deer
bá-mo cow
jo-mo milch yak
p'ág hog
luk sheep
khyi-dá dog
alü cat
búlakhá sable
p'o calf
jágma squirrel
demo bear
beu (byu) snake
p'yá any bird
bep frog
nyam-yo cricket
p'yá-wang bat
zigmo porcupine

Things Eatable.

Chá tea
ṭá-leb loaf
khu cake
shurbu dough-balls in tea or soup
to or *to-zá* victuals, dinner
om milk
gongdo eggs
már butter
ṭ'ukpa broth
shá-chuk dry meat
lug-shá mutton
chum rice
khim p'yá fowl
nyá fish
chháng beer
khye-chháng murwar beer
chhu water
kyur-ru vinegar
toma potato
tárulbák yam
dowa artichoke
khámbu peach
ts'á lumpa orange
kye-dong plaintain
ts'erlum raspberry
kára sugar
ts'á salt

House and its Contents.

khim house
nyuk-khim house of bamboo
shing-khim hut of wood
do-chhál the pavement
gom door
kháng-mik room
gyá-kár window
entar floor
mi fire
chenṭ'e table
gyáṭ'i chair
shu-ten cushion-seat
chhá cupboard
nye-sá bed
khyu-zhong bathing tub
de-cho W. C.
chumi lamp
p'orpa bowl
loknyo spoon
ki-chhung knife
káryo cup
derma dish
tse-o basket
chhá-li blanket
chhámpin teapot
dom box
pálla-túla scales
p'e-kyal flour-bag
sáng cooking-kettle, degchi
te-ko wash-basin
shel (glass in window, &c.)
khyimtse scissors
p'ákze brush

Natural Objects.

nyim sun
dau moon
kâm star
humpo cloud
ri mountain
gang hill-spur
káng-chen glacier
rong ravine
sá-ru landslip
khá-ru snow-slip
t'okpo deep gorge
lam-t'ang cliff-ledge
t'okzár torrent-bed
chháb rain
chhu-wo river
tsâ grass
shing tree
mintok flower
kyá-ma fern
do stone
mukpa fog
kâng snow
khyâkrom ice
tâk rock
shá-mo fungus
söke shâmo mush-room
shing-gi dâma tree-leaf
chhâ-rá evergreen oak
pá-ma cypress
gomrok holly
shukpa juniper
yâli maple
gyi dong india-rubber tree
kyön-me shing pine tree
dum-po tree-trunk

Miscellaneous.

chhö khá thing
ming name
lu song
ur noise
lob-bön teacher
yig khang school
t'om market
sátá map
rin price
kyá hair
go head
gyáb back
tö-pa belly
dempo cheek
mi-dŏ eye
námcho ear
lé-dum leg
lak-ko arm
ná nose
sei gold
gü silver
yi-ge a letter
chho book
khyá blood
hlam boot
torma trousers
shambu cap
ko-lák coat

III.—ADJECTIVES.

The adjective invariably follows its noun; and when the noun is thus qualified by an adjective the proper case-sign is affixed to the latter only, *e.g.*

P'iru noksu chi: a dark night.

Pötso tsok kyi lak di: the hand of a dirty boy.

Pu lem chu: a good son.

Where the adjective is used as an attribute, the article is often placed before as well as after the noun; *e.g.*

P'i-ru di noksu be
or *Di p'i-ru di noksu be* } The night is dark.

Here is the adjective as a single attribute:
Ngá t'ang chhé-po yin: I am tired.

The adjective is rendered more intense by various words placed *before* it:—*há-chang* or *nyogi* = much, very. *Mám* = very. But these are properly adverbs.
Tá di há chang nyambu du': The horse is very quiet.
Rin di há-chang be: The price is too much.
Di nyim di nyogi t'üm-po be: The sun is very hot.
Tá-to nyogi khyá bo be: It is very cold now.

COMPARISON OF ADJECTIVES.

"Greater" is rendered *te-le chhe* "than that, great."
"Stronger" " " *te-le she* "than that, strong."

Pá-shing audi te-le she min du': This pole is not stronger than that.

"Strongest" is rendered *gün le she* "than all, strong."

Zok p'idi gün le t'o be. That crag is the highest.

Tse-o di lo riyung audi le ringkyam chi go be: The basket requires a longer tie-rope than that: (*lit:* To the basket, than that tie-rope, a long is wanting.)
The comparative form of sentence may be slightly varied by the insertion of the word *yang* after the particle *le* which stands for "than."

My heart is heavier than my load: *Nge sem di nge toi di le yang ji-chen be*

A common superlative expletive is *chhok*
This is the best: *audi lem chhok be.*
This way is the shortest: *Di lam di t'ung kyám chhok be.*

Some Ordinary Adjectives.

Lem good	*chhempo* or *chhe* great, large
Málep bad	*chhung* small
yákpo good } of actions and	*nyok-ma* muddy
wákpo bad } things.	*tsok* dirty
shempa young	*tsanmo* clean
ge-po old	*noksu* dark
nyom-chhung poor	*wö-chen* light
ji-chen heavy	*khé-ta* or *khésta* clever
yáng-ke or *yáng-mo* light	*shé* strong
jam tong easy	*shé-chhung* weak
jâm-po soft	*gyoba* fast
takia hard	*bul-po* slow
kyáng all, the whole	*bom-po* thick
sarpo fresh, new	*sim-bu* thin (slender)
nying-po old, not new	*zhengchen* broad
t'ümpo hot	*zhengmé* narrow
kyá-bo cold	*máp* red
ring-kyam long	*nák-po* black
t'ung-kyam short	*káp* white
kom-bo dry	*serpo* yellow
bong-bo wet	*leb-leb* flat
lo-chen lazy	*dálchen* quiet, smooth
dze-pa pretty	*kyur-po* sour

IV.—PRONOUNS.

1. Personal Pronouns :—These are subject to inflection of case as nouns and adjectives are.

Ngá or *ngá-rang* I ; *nge* of me, my ; *ngá-lo*, me, to me ; *ngaī* by me.

Chhö You ; *Chhö-kyi* of you, your ; *Chhö-lo* you, to you ; *Chhö Kyī* by you.

Kho : he ; *Kho-i* of him, his ; *Kho-lo* to him, him ; *Kho-yī* by him.

Mo : she ; *Mo-i* of her, hers ; *Mo-lo* to her, her ; *Mo-yī* by her.

Di : It ; *Di-kyi* of it ; *Di-lo* it, to it.

The use of *mo* as the feminine third personal pronoun is not universal, and *kho* in many parts of Sikkim as always in Tibet represents both "he" and "she."

In many districts *ngá-rang* is always used in preference to *nga.*

Examples :—

Chhö pum lem be: You are a good girl.

Kho pŏtso málep be: He is a bad boy.

Chhö-kyi mi-do tsum: Shut your eyes.

Kho ngá-lo gong-do gu ts'ong she'in: He will sell me nine eggs.

Mo-i kyà ring-kyàm du': Her hair is long.

Ngà-rang cho-li dàma sá do'in: I am eating cho-li leaves.

b.—A curious point in the use of the possessive case of these pronouns must be noted. The noun may be accompanied by both the possessive pronoun and the definite article.

Nge dôm di bā shok: Bring my box.

This is literally: "Bring the my box;" but the construction evidently arises from the pronoun being treated as a noun in the genitive case, and if a noun were to be substituted for the pronoun the above form would be perfectly regular. The rendering is really; Bring the box of me. The employment of this article in such cases seems often to be left to the choice of the speaker or else is ruled by the general custom in each individual instance. However the article must be used in this way where the intention is to particularise any thing belonging to a person as apart from the property of others. Where no stress is laid upon the ownership the article, may be omitted, *e.g.*

Moi pu shi song du': her son has died.

Moi pu di ngá-lo ten nang: Show me her son

Again :—

Di-kyi rin di nyogi be: The price of it is much.

N.B.—The pronoun *di* it, stands for "this" when the latter is used apart from any expressed noun, and is varied to *te* for "that" when similarly occurring.

2. Demonstrative Pronouns—Although we have appended the foregoing note to the preceding section, we find the article *di* often loosely conjoined to a noun to indicate both "this" and "that." In classical Tibetan we find the same practice; but, in the colloquial dialect of Sikkim, provision has been properly made for distinguishing the demonstrative pronouns from the mere definite article. The pronouns themselves are

Audi: this. *P'idi:* that.

However where we should ordinarily say "that" we frequently find *audi* is the pronoun used. The fact is, this usage really arises from the accuracy with which Tibetans (in common with other orientals) employ their demonstrative pronouns to discriminate at once the proximity or distance in situation of the thing indicated. We on the contrary generally use "this" or "that" almost indiscriminately and more in relation to the priority of the time of mentioning a thing than in reference to its actual place. In fact

Audi = this here; *P'i-di* = that yonder

These pronouns are used both when conjoined to nouns and when pure *pro-nouns, e.g.*

Audi ke-kyi khim bo? Whose house is this (*or* "that near here")

Khim audi ke bo? Whose is this house?

Chhö audi kam p'yà du': Why are you doing that? (properly *this*)

Ngà-lo gom-pa p'idi nangsha ta go: I want to see within that temple (yonder)

[We may usefully construe the last sentence. *Nga-lo* to me, *go* it is necessary *ta (she)* to see *nàng-sha* within *gompa p'idi* that temple.]

In numerous instances, as in the case of the personal pronouns, the definite article is used in conjunction with the demonstrative pronoun. The latter is then placed before instead of after the noun, *e.g.*

Audi ki-chhung di nyogi ring-kyàm du': That knife is very long, (near at hand.)

Audi dom di yà-te bàksong: Take that box up-stairs.

Ngá-lo audi den di mingo: I don't want this carpet.

Where there is an interrogative pronoun also, the *di* by custom is placed after the latter: *e.g.*

Audi pum ka di bo: Who is this girl?

3. RELATIVE PRONOUNS.—These which hardly occur at all in literary Tibetan are perhaps altogether absent from Dái-jong ke', except in a few correlative phrases which need not be particularised here. However all the purposes of our relative pronouns are fitly compassed by means of participial clauses. The participial clause is introduced immediately in front of what would in English be the antecedent of the relative pronoun, and stands as if it were a huge compound adjective qualifying the antecedent noun to which it refers. Thus the sentence, "The man who lived in that house died yesterday" would take the form: "The living-in-that-house man died yesterday." Here "living-in-that-house" is the big adjective qualifying "man." In literary Tibetan this participial clause might be placed, like any ordinary adjective, either following the noun to which it was related, or else before it with the participle

of this clause inflected in the genitive case. In the Sikkim colloquial the latter alternative seems to be the only admissable practice, the genitive inflexion being, however, dispensed with.

The participle is formed by merely affixing the syllable *khen* to the root of the verb; and, save in a few exceptional instances, we find no difference in expression between the present and past participle. The context must determine the time to the English speaker; for the Tibetan sees no necessity to discriminate between a present and a past in mere dependent clauses. Thus we have:—*ts'ong-nyi* to sell; *ts'ong khen*, selling, who sells; *ts'ong khen*, having sold, who sold.

The participles passive would even be loosely rendered by the very same expressions as the foregoing; although if precision were required we should probably find the distinction marked by the addition of *zhe'* or *kyap* to the verbal root, thus:—*ts'ong zhe' khen* being sold, which is sold; *ts'ong zhe' khen* having been sold, which was sold, which had been sold. *Kyap* is used only with certain verbs. "Had been sold" might be further discriminated by the insertion of *song*, thus: *ts'ong song zhe khen;* but this compound would only be used where particular stress as to time and manner of the transaction was thought to be desirable.

EXAMPLES OF RELATIVE CLAUSES.

a. Chhö tásong nyo khen òm-di nga-lo ná. Give me the milk which you brought this morning.

β. Khim lo lug bak yong khen shempa di-yī potso-i hlam ku bák song: The butcher who brought the sheep to the house stole the boy's boots.

(N. B. *Shempa di yī* the instrumental case as given in this sentence is grammatically correct; but commonly, as we have sufficiently shewn, the nom. is always used and thus the *yī* would most likely not be said.)

γ. Konchhok lo de-pá kye khen di nga nyinpo kya-nyi. I want to love those who have faith in God.

δ. Di p'iru kyáng àb khen khyi-da di sung-khyi malep be. The dog who barks all night is a bad watch-dog.

(Here we find the definite article placed at the commencement and close of the relative clause, thus neatly marking it off. This is only an expansion of a similar use of the article already noticed in § I.)

4.—INTERROGATIVE PRONOUNS.—These are *ká* who, *kan* or *kam* which, what, *kambe* why, *ke* or *ke-kyi* whose, *ke-nái* from whom? All such are sufficiently illustrated under § V. 6 and 8.

V.—THE VERB.

We find in the Sikkim colloquial a fairly systematic method of expressing the various phases of the verb. In fact the tenses are particularised in this dialect with greater accuracy and regularity than are to be found in the book language of Tibet. Some variety in the affixes appended to the verbal roots is met with according to the locality of the speakers. In the Darjiling and Kalimpong districts we find certain strange affixes which disappear as we proceed north of Tumlong. On the Tibetan frontier moreover the verbal inflections assimilate entirely with those peculiar to Tsang. We believe however the southern manner of inflexion to be that proper to the Sikkim dialect and to be generally comprehendible to natives and itinerants in the northern districts. Nevertheless all variations shall be noted below.

1. INFINITIVE.—This is formed by adding *nyi* or *she* to the root of the verb, e.g., *káp-she* or *káp-nyi* to cover. *Shé* is the usual affix throughout Tsang and equally common in Sikkim. *Nyi* is peculiar to the Darjiling district.

2. FUTURE TENSE.—From the Infinitive the future tense is formed by adding *'in* (really *yin*) for the first person and sometimes *du' (duk)* for the 2nd and 3rd person. But usually when the 3rd person future has to be expressed the regular Tibetan future, formed by the addition of *ong* not to the infinitive but the root is resorted to.

Examples will make this sufficiently understood.

I shall drink : { *Ngá t'ung she 'in.* or *Ngá t'ung nyi 'in.*

He will drink { *Kho t'ung ong.* or *kho t'ung she du'.*

Ong becomes *yong* in northern Sikkim as in Tibet. Elsewhere always *ong* as in Balti.

The formation of the future from the infinitive, it will be noted, is very natural; for *'in* = am, du' = is. So we have *t'ung-she* to drink; *t'ung she 'in* am to drink = will drink; *t'ung-she du'* is to drink = will drink.

3. PRESENT TENSE.—The root with *do 'in* annexed (probably *du' 'in* or *duk yin*) is generally heard when the first person occurs. The root with *chen du'* or *chen be'* for the 2nd and 3rd persons. Thus—

I am eating rice: *Ngá chum-lo sá do 'in.*

He is coming home: *Kho khim-lo ong chen du'.*

You are beating the horse very much } *Chhö tá di lo nyoji dung chen du'.*

He runs like a horse: *Kho tá dendá chăng be.*

4. PERFECT TENSES.—The past definite form generally can be expressed by the root of the verb with *zhe*, *che*, or *j'he* (variously sounded) annexed. The past indefinite requires *song zhe* or *song du'*. Thus—

He wrote a letter: *kho yige chi p'i zhe.*

He has written a letter: *kho yige chi p'i song du'.*

Sometimes with *du'* alone:

Mo zung du' she seized, did seize.

Mo or *mo-i chhak du'*: She broke

There seems no decided distinction between active and passive voices: *chhak song du'* has been broken; but *gyu chung* often indicates the Passive, e.g., *sa gyu chung* has been eaten.

Certain styles are preferred for certain verbs. Thus *shi she* to die, always forms the past tense with *song.*

shi song, died; *shi song zhe* has (quite) died, is dead.

shi song du' did die (emphatic)

t'ong che, saw; *t'ong song zhe* has seen

Other verbs have special past forms:—

gyu-she, to go; *song* went

bak do nyi, to take, take away; *bák song zhe* has taken.

p'ya-she, to do; *zhe* or *che*: did; *zhe song* has done.

And a few others.

5. IMPERATIVE.—The simple root; or else the root with *tang* and, as a politer form, with *nang* or *nyá* added.

Eat this: *andi sá.* Open the door: *yom-di p'i!* Cook food: *to tso tang!*

Please show the way: *lam di ten-náng.*

Please give me a rupee: *nga-lo tiruk chi p'in nang* or *p'in tang.*

6. POTENTIAL MOOD.—The root, or sometimes the infinitive, with *chhug* or *ts'uk* annexed. The latter form is the real verb, *chhug* or *chhuk* being the provincial pronunciation of the *ts'uk.*

I can run quickly: *Nyá gyobá chang ts'uk.*

He can climb up the tree: *Kho shing di dzek chhuk.*

The interrogative form is most frequently used and differs from the ordinary interrogatives to be explained hereafter:—

Can you read the book: *Chhö chho di dok ts'uk-ká?*

Can you see the gentleman: *Chhö kusho di t'ong chhug-gá?*

Is he able to use a gun: *Kho mindá chi kyi p'ent'o p'yá she chhug-ga?*

Are you able to fight: *Chhö t'abmo kyap chhug-ga?*

Can the boy sing a song: *Potso di lu kyap ts'uk-ka?*

NOTE TO PAGE 21.

In all verbs the Plural Number is exactly the same as the Singular, so far as the verb itself is concerned; but the pronoun may be altered in the 1st and 3rd persons Plural where any stress is laid upon the Number:—

SINGULAR.	PLURAL.
Ngá or *ngárang 'in:* I am.	*Ngáchá 'in:* We are.
Chhö or *chhörang be:* Thou art.	*Chhö be:* You are.
Kho or *khorang be:* He is.	*Khong be:* / *Khong-ts'o be:* } They are.

7.—The Substantive Verb.

Ngá 'in: I am, *Chhö be* Thou art, you are, *Kho be* He is. An alternative form of *be* is *me*, found occurring after the vowel o.

I am very wet: *Ngá nyogi bong-bo 'in.*

You are a bad girl: *Chhö pum málep be.*

The book is easy to read: *Di chho di dok-nyi jam-tong be.*

You are a clean boy: *Chhö potso tsang-mo me.*

You are a filthy girl: *Chhö pum tsok be.*

He is an idle man: *Khö mi shé-lo me.*

The woman is pretty and dirty: *Di pum di dzebo tárung málebo be.*

We find occasionally *du'* substituted for *be* by the more Tibetanized folk.

That girl is my wife: *Audi-pum di nge-kyermán du'.*

That pretty girl is to be my wife: *Pum dzebo audi nge kyermán chung she du'.*

She is unmarried: *Mo menshar du'.*

The interrogative form of the verb "to be" runs thus:—

Ngá yö' ta: am I? *Chhö bo*: are you? *Kho bo*: is he?

A common alternative form of *bo* is *mo.*

Where are you? *Chhö ká-khá mo?*

Who is that lama behind the house: *Audi lama khim di se-lo di ka mo?*

Are you young: *Chhö shempa bo?*

Is the horse cold: *Tá di k'yábo mo?*

Where is the man who came here yesterday } *Nai khásong ong khen mi-di ka-khá be?* or *ka-kha bo?*

Who is out there: *P'ạ-ki p'ila ká mo?*

8. The Possessive verb "to have."—As in Russian, Hindustani, and many other languages the possessive verb is rendered by the circumlocution. "There is near——" or "to—— there is." Thus: "I have three children" becomes "To me three children are" "*Nga-lo p'ugu sum be.*" Again: "you have a warm dry coat" is best turned "near you a warm dry coat is" "*Chhö za ko-lák t'um-po kombo du'.*" Interrogatively: "Have you three children" *Chhö lo p'ugu sum-bo?* "Have you any boots to sell?" *Chhö za di ts'ong khen hlam kan di bo?* Here note how the double article *di—di* is used to bind the participle ts'ong-khen to its proper antecedent.

Where "have" is a simple auxilliary joined to another verb, it is usually represented by *du.*'

9. GENERAL INTERROGATIVES.—These are usually rendered by the addition of the interrogatives auxilliary *bo* or *mo* to the proper tense of the verb required. Thus

Did you go to the bazaar yesterday: *chhö khá-sáng t'om lo song bo?*

What will you sell me: *Chhö ngá-lo kan ts'ong she mo?*

Are you drinking beer: *chhö chháng t'ung do bo?*

Are you bringing the dog: *chhö khyi-da di bák nang bo?*

Except when it is the verb substantive the interrogative particle is sometimes omitted if an interrogative pronoun occurs:—

Why are you doing that: *chhö audi kumbe p'yá du'?*

When did you arrive: *chhö nam leb sang?*

With the potential auxilliary "to be able" the interrogative particle is never heard:—

Can you read: *chhö dok chhug-ga?*

Can you come to-morrow: *chhö t'orang ong ts'uk-ka?*

By custom the particle is abridged into "o" with certain verbs ending in k (really g).

Why did you break the cup: *chhö káryö' di kam chhak-ko.*

Where have you put the oranges: *chhö ts'á-lumpa di ká-na zháko?*

Have you read it: *chhö di-lo doko?*

10. NEGATIVES.—Are expressed by the particle *ma* with the perfect or imperative and by *mi* with the present or future tenses.

Don't talk nonsense: *chhol-khá ma lap!*

He did not give me one rupee: *kho ngá-lo tiruk-chi' p'in má che.*

The girl will not come with me: *Pum di ngá nyambu ong nyi min* (or *m'ong nyi 'in.)*

He will not bite: *kho so tap mi ong.*

He is not reading your book: *kho chhö-kyi chho di dok chen mi du'.*

He is not eating now: *Tá-to sá do min.*

It will be observed from the above examples that the negative is either compounded with the auxilliary member of any verb or placed immediately preceding the last syllable of the verb. With the past tense the latter course is always pursued: e.g., *kho shi mi song*: He has not died. With the infinitive form of the verb we find the negative placed last: e.g.

The idle man has nothing to eat: *mi shélo di sa nyi mi.*

11. PARTICIPLES.—The syllable *khen* added to the verbal root forms the participle. This important branch of the verb is fully illustrated under § iv, 3.

12. GERUNDS.—These are formed by the addition of certain brief particles to the verb of the gerundial clause. These particles are *te* (often vulgarly *ti*), *ne*, *táng*, and *par* or *war*.

a.—The first two are commonly employed to express clauses such as in English are introduced by the words "when," "as," "having." Examples will best illustrate our meaning:—

Having eaten his food, he desired the remainder: *Ri-kyi to di sa song-te hlak-ma dö zhe du'.*

(*N. B.—Ri-kyi* is here used for *kho-i* because the possessor is also the acting subject of the sentence. § iv, 1, *b.*)

When you have done, come to me: *chhö-kyī zhe song-ne nga-lo shok.*

(*Chhö-kyī* is the agentive case which should always be used with transitive verbs instead of the nom. case; but colloquially the rule is only in a few such instances as the present one commonly observed. *Zhe song* is the past tense of *p'ya she* to do).

Go and fetch it (i.e., "going, fetch it"): *song-te di-lo bàk shok.*

(This form is exactly parallel to the Hindustani *jákar usko le-ao*).

b.—*Tang* joined to the infinitive best interprets short dependent clauses:—

On my firing the gun, three men fell: *nga mindá kyap pa tang mi sum tung song.*

(*Kyap-pa* is the Tibetan form of the infinitive which in our dialect should be *kyap-she;* yet this is the form we generally hear with *tang*, which, be it noted, invariably requires the infinitive when used as a gerundial particle).

Hearing you call, I came: *chhö kē kyap-ne ngá nyen-pa tang ong zhe.* (*Lit:* "you calling, I on hearing came.")

Looking down the kud, I saw the man lying: *kad di teng-lo tá-ne ngá di nye khen mi di t'ong zhe.*

c.—We find *par* or *war* joined to the repeated root to express concurrent clauses introduced in English by the word "while."

While I am sleeping, don't make a noise: *ngá nye nye par ur má kyap.*

While I am going to the market, you must dig up the artichokes: *ngá t'om lo gyu gyu war chhörang do-wa ko go.*

While I am gone, watch: *nyá song song par kug tang.*

This section may be concluded by the enumeration of certain of the more commonly occurring verbs.

P'in-she to give
ná-nyi to bestow
gyu-she to go
dul-nyi to walk
chang-she to run
gyuk-she to run
ong-nyi to come
sá-nyi to eat
t'ung-she to drink
tungshe to fall
küm gha nyi to choke
nye-she to lie down
nyá' do nyi to sleep
dö or *dü nyi* to sit, or remain
nyo-nyi to buy
ts'ong-she to sell
khyu-she to wash, bathe
dok-she to read
pi-she to write
p'i-she to open
tsum she to shut
dzung-she to consider
dzung-she to hold
káp-she to cover
nyen-she to listen, hear
khá nyen she to obey
bák ong nyi to bring
bák nang nyi to fetch
bák gyu nyi to take away

T'ong-she to see
dung-she to beat
ko-tung she to throw away
ten-nyi to show
tá-nyi to look at
kön-nyi to wear, put on
zhák she to place, put
p'yá nyi to do, make
tsuk nyi to strike, push
ts'uk she to be able
chhug-she to be able
t'ob-she to obtain
ko-nyi to dig
kyap-she to throw
ngoshi she to know
gü she to stay, wait
shi nyi to die
lap-she to speak
ser-she to tell, to name
gá deb she to laugh
gyo do shor she to laugh
go-she to want
t'abmo kyap she to fight
né kyap she to become ill
tok-nyi to cut
dzek she to climb
lem she to crush
den she to pull, draw.
sik she to hoist, shove up.

VI.—ADVERBS.

1. In the Sikkim colloquial we find no distinction made between the adjective and its corresponding adverb. Thus *jámpo*=both "soft" and "softly;" *sarpo*="new" and "afresh" "newly;" *jam-tong*="easily" and "easy."

However, in addition to the adverbs derived from adjectives, there are in use a number of primitive adverbs, both simple and compound—adverbs of Time and Place.

A few of these may be noted here.

"Always" is rendered by *át'ang mache*; "often" by *át'ang*.

"Never" is expressed by *ná-mo* or *ná-mong* and a negative before the verb, thus:

Ngá ná-mo chhá-khá málep mi ts'ong: I never sell bad things.

Other temporal adverbs are *gyob* soon, *lok-te* again, *mölá* immediately, *har* suddenly, *tá-to* now, *táchi* lately, and *se-lo* afterwards. Also those in connection with the measurement of time:—

Tá-ring to-day; *tásong* this morning; *táring p'iru* to-night. *Khásang* yesterday; *dong* last night; *nyim-kyang* all day. *Ngáru:* to-morrow (morning); *t'orang* to-morrow.

Adverbs of Place:—*Nái* here, *p'áki* yonder, *hákyi* there *p'ina*, in front, *t'ekyá-lo* straight on, forward, *má-ki* below, at bottom, *khor* round, *khor khor* around, *pang khá* outside, *nang-khá* inside.

2. INTERROGATIVE ADVERBS.—These are *nam* when, *ká-khá* where, *ká-na* whither, where, *ká-lái* whence, *jhi-tar* how, in what way, *ká-dem* how, *ká dzü (mo)* how much, *tu-tu* how many. They are employed precisely as the interrogative pronouns; in the sentence generally standing next before the verb. (See § v, 9.) Examples:—

Dum-rá náng-shá zigmo tu-tu t'ong song bo: How many porcupines did you see in the garden?

Kho nam shi song zhe: When did he die?

VII.—POSTPOSITIONS.

These are simple and compound; the first being merely the case signs already enumerated. On the former however a few remarks may be made here. *Lo*, the dative and accus affix rarely signifies "to" except after verbs meaning "to give." The locative *ná* is of course the proper affix to use in these cases where we should say "at" or "to." However for "at" the post position *zá*="near" is sometimes employed, just as *pás* is used in Hindustani. The best form for "from" is lé (pronounced lái in Tsang.) The Tibetan *terminative* case is hardly heard at all in southern Sikkim.

Compound Post positions are very frequent. The chief are these:—

náng-shá or *ná-shá*	in, into.	*tandá le*	because of, on account of
		se-lo	behind, after.
ten-le	for, instead of.	*dün-tu*	before.
teng-khá or *khá*	on, upon.	*khá-wak*	under, beneath
teng-lo.	down.	*nyam-bo*	with, along with
dem	like, such as.	*sán-te*	up to, unto.

On the above let us remark: *teng-khá* is sometimes used for "up," *e.g. Shing di teng-khá dzek*: climb up the tree; *sánte* when combined with a negative is the method of expressing "until." The latter usage is worthy of note. Thus: "I shall wait until you return" is rendered *chhö lokté má ong sán-te ngá gü she'in.* Often we hear this as *chhö lok mong sánte ngá gü she'in.* Again: Walk on until you see a bamboo house *chhö nyuk khim chi ma t'ong sánte long dul.* Literally of course this would express the reverse of what is really understood, namely "Until you do not see a bamboo house, walk on. "When *sánte* has the signification of "as far as" or "to" the negative does not occur.

Properly all the compound postpositions govern the genitive case and ought to be preceded by nouns so inflected; but in practice such a rule is rarely if ever observed, the simple nouns or adjective standing uninflected and followed by the governing postposition. *e.g.*,

Khim náng-shá song: Go in the house.

Ngá tiruk nyi p'in she 'in khyi-dá di tándá le: I will give two rupees for the dog.

VIII.—CONJUNCTIONS.

Rarely used; the gerundial affixes usually supplying their place when coupling clauses or sentences together. Thus "Go and tell him" becomes "going, tell him" *song-ti kho-lo ser* just as in Hindustani we should say *Jákar ussiko bolo!* "Come and look:" *Ong-ti ta!*

A copulative conjunction for coupling nouns is, however, in use: *Tárung*=and, e.g., *khy-i-da tárung dlü* dog and cat. When no stress is laid on the conjunction it is readily omitted: *ngá lo mar gongdo cha bák shok* Bring me butter, eggs and tea. *Tárung* means really "still more" "yet."

The conjunction "if" is rendered by *nu* placed after the verb, as in the following sentence:

Nyim kyang yige dok nu, chhö-kyi mik suk kyap ong: If you read all day, your eyes will ache (feel pain).

Chhö mi lem yin-nu, ngá dung she 'in : If you are not good, I shall beat (you).

Chhö au-dem gyobá sá tákye nu, kyöm ghá ong : If you continue eating so fast, you will choke.

Sometimes the regular Tibetan form *ná* is employed instead of the corrupted form *nu*. Moreover every Daijong man would, when writing, put *ná* not *nu*.

ALTHOUGH is expressed by *rung* placed similarly to *nu*. Thus :—

Chhö né kyi kyap rung, sá go be : Though you are ill, you must eat.

Kho nyim ts'án kyang sa rung, ná-mo gyak-shá mi ong : Although he ate all day and night, he would never become fat.

(Note here the absence of "and" between *nyim* and *ts'án* ; also use of *na-mo* with negative for "never.")

When *rung* occurs with the verb "to be," the intensive form of that verb is generally resorted to namely the Tibetan *mod-pa* to be indeed, sounded *mö'pa* :

Ri-kyi ro di dur nang-sha mö-pa rung chhö lok-te lang nyi 'in : Though your body is indeed in the grave you shall rise again.

IX.—FORMATIVES.

What is treated of in Grammars under the head of "Derivation" may be very briefly disposed of here.

1.—Certain adjectives are formed or "derived" from nouns by the addition of the syllable *chen* to the noun, e. g., *rin* price, *rin-chen* expensive ; *ts'erma* thorn, *ts'erma-chen* thorny, prickly ; *khyo* anger, *khyo-chen* angry ; *khyá* blood, *khyá-chen* bloody. In fact most of our adjectives ending in "y" or "ous" are formed in Dé-jong Ké thus from substantives.

The negative formative corresponding to *chen* is *mé* "without"

2.—The affix *chhok* added to a verbal root goes to form those adjectives which signify capability of suffering anything, or fitness for being made use of. *Sá-nyi* to eat, *sá-chhok* eatable ; *t'ong she* to see, *t'ong chhok* visible, capable of being seen, *chhak-she* to break, *chhák-chhok* breakable, &c. The negative form takes *mi*, as *t'ong mi chhok* invisible.

3.—A third formative is *khen* signifying chiefly the doer of any action, much akin to the Hindustani *wala ;* as *p'yá-khen* doer, maker, *dok-khen* reader, *bák-khen* carrier. Like *wala* added also to substantives ; as *toi* a load, *toi-khen* bearer of a load, *hlam khen* bootmaker, *tá-khen* a groom, sa'is.

NUMERALS.

Chi	one	chu-chi	eleven
Nyi	two	chu-ṅyi	twelve
Sum	three	chu-sum	thirteen
Zhi	four	chub-zhi	fourteen
Nga	five	chenga	fifteen
Tuk	six	chu-tuk	sixteen
Dŭin	seven	chub-dŭin	seventeen
Gye	eight	chegye	eighteen
Gu	nine	chu-gu	nineteen
Chu-tamba	ten	khe-chik	twenty

Sum-chu tamba	thirty
So-chi	thirty-one
So-nyi, &c.	thirty-two, &c.
Zhib-chu tamba :	forty
Zhe-chi, &c.	forty-one, &c.
Nga-chu	fifty
Khe-sum	sixty
Re-chi	sixty-one
Re-nyi, &c.	sixty-two
Gya-chi	one hundred
Tong-rok	thousand

DAYS OF THE WEEK.

Sá-nyim :	Sunday
Sá-dou :	Monday
Sá-mikmá :	Tuesday
Sá-hlák-bo :	Wednesday
Sá-p'urbo :	Thursday
Sá-pásúng :	Friday
Sá-p'embo :	Saturday.

Nái sá p'embo shok : come here on Saturday.
Chhö lo ka dzü som-bo : How old are you?
Nga-lo khe chik 'm : I am twenty years' old.

COLLOQUIAL SENTENCES.

NOTE.—These sentences are nearly all in the Sikkim colloquial or Dé-jong Ké. Accordingly when Tibetans from beyond the Jé-lep, Donkya, Kangla, and other passes, are communicated with, the following rules may be observed: For *be* (is, are) use *du'* or *yin;* for *bo* or *mo* say *du'ká* or *yö-tam* or *yin-ná*. *Bák song* and *bák sho'* should be avoided, and *khyer song* "take away" and *khyer sho'* "bring," should be substituted. The future tense may be rendered by means of *yong* or *gyu du'* added to the verbal root: *ten yong* "will shew," *dzek gyu du'* "will climb." *Song* for the past tense is very universal, but *chung* or *jhung* is the commoner affix in Central Tibet, *e.g.*, *Ná-la di náng jhung du'*: "The rent has been paid;" but in Sikkim colloquial: *Ná-la di p'in song zhe.*

BRIEF ORDERS.

Come here :	Nái shok !
Come back	Lokte shok !
Come with me	Nge nyambu shok !
Come near me	Nge tsar-ka (or "zà") shok !
Come to-morrow	T'orang-ra shok !
Speak slowly	Kulup lap !
Go away :	Long song !
Go at once :	Hlem song !
Go to the market :	T'om na song !
Go and fetch some water :	*Song ne chhu atsiche bak shok !*
Go outside :	*Pang kha song !*
Go and tell him what I say :	*Song ne nga ser khen di lap !*
Go home again :	*Khim-na lok song !*
Go further :	*P'ar-tsami song*
Go gently :	*Kále song*
Bring me some tea :	*Cha nga-lo bák shok*
Bring more water :	*Chhu yáng-kyár bák shok*
Fetch the horse here :	Tà di nái t'i.
Take away those things :	*Chha-ka di ták bák song !*
Take the coat and dry it :	Di kolak di bak song di kam bá shok.
Throw it away :	Di t'u ko tang !
Send word (Give notice)	Lon ser !
Send him here :	Kho-lo nài tong.
Make haste :	*Gyo bá p'yá !*
Take care :	*U'ip !*
Be steady (or careful) :	*Riko gyimbo*
Sit down now :	*Tá-to dü !*
Remain here :	Nài gü !
Say that again :	Lok te lap
Don't tell a lie :	Dzun ma kyap !
Open the door :	Gom di p'i.
Put my box on the ground :	Ngé dom di sa zhàk.
Climb up that hill and look :	P'idi gang-di dzek nài tà !

USEFUL QUESTIONS.

Can you speak Hindustani :	Chhö Hindu kyi ké lap ts'ug-ga ?
Can you speak English :	Chhö Ingrezi ké lap ts'ug-ga ?
Do you know that man :	Chhö kyī mi p'idi ngoshi bo ?
Who is this boy :	Potso audi kà mo
What are you doing :	Chhö kam p'ya du'
Why are you doing that :	Chhö audi dem kambe p'ya du
Why are you asking :	Chhö kam-be t'e du'
When did you see him :	Chhö kho-lo nam t'ong bo ?
Where did you see it :	Chhö di-lo ka-khà t'ong bo ?

Look! do you see him:	Ta! chhö kho-lo t'ong be bo?
Is he dead:	Kho shi song zhe bo?
Where have you been:	Chhö ka-khà song zhe?
Can you write a letter:	Chhö yi-ge chi p'i she ts'ug-ga?
What do you want:	Chhö kan go she bo?
What is his name:	Kho-yi ming kà de'su
Where do you live:	Chhö ka-khà dü-do mo? (or dü-to bo?)
Will he come back soon:	Kho ma-la lok hleb she bo?
Can she carry this load:	Mo toi di bak ts'ug-ga
Where have you put my boots:	Chhö nge hlam ka-na zhàko
Where have I put my keys:	Nga ri-kyi dimi ka-na zhàko?
Who are you? What name:	Chhö ka mo? ming kam bo?

ON A JOURNEY.

Make everything ready for starting:	Chhà-kha kyang gyuk tok.
Pack up the tent:	Ugūr t'altik p'yà
Roll up the rugs:	Chhà-li di gyil p'yà
Fasten that bundle more securely than that:	Di t'um-po di te le t'ang dam
You carry the tent-poles:	Chhö gur-shing bak song!
That is your load:	Audi chhö-kyi toi di du'
Your load is not heavy:	Chhö kyi toi di min du'
Now we must set off:	Ta-to gyu go
It is time to go:	Gyu-gyi tüi cho be
Go in front: I will walk behind you:	P'ina song; ngarang chhö kyi so-le gyu she 'in
Lift up that box:	Di dom di ya t'o
Turn the horse round:	Tà di khor kyap
Walk quickly:	Gyoba dul
Hold the bridge firmly:	Sampa di tángpo chhin
You go over the bridge first:	Chhö sam tengkha p'ina gyu
Are you tired:	Chhö t'ang-chhe-po nya
We have not travelled far:	Ngacha t'a ringkyam ma song
I am tired:	Nga t'ang-chhe-po yin
You can climb as quickly as a horse:	Chhö tà chi da denda dzek ts'uk (or chhuk) be
Carry that slowly up the hill:	Di chhà-kha di gang tengkha ku-lup bak song
Tell him to come here quickly:	Kho-lo gyoba nái shok lap
That leech is sucking your blood:	Audi pü-po di chhö-kyi khya jip chen du'
Sit down:	Sà dü
Go into that house and buy some food:	Khim audi nàng-sha song-te to à-tsi -chi nyoba sho'
Do you see many leeches on this grass:	Chhö pü-po nyogi tsà audi teng-kha t'ong-ga.

Do you see any leeches on my leg :	Chhö pü-po à-tsi-chi nge lé-dum tengkha t'ong-ga ?
How far can you walk :	Chhö t'à ring t'ung kà dzoi gyu ts'uk ?

ASKING THE WAY

Whose house is that :	Khim audi ke bo ?
What is the name of the village :	Yults'o kyi ming kà mo ?
Is that a temple on the hill :	P'idi gompa gang tengkha di bo ?
Show me the way to Nga-tong :	Nga-tong-kyi lam di nga-lo ten nang .
Say that again :	Lok-te lap
Speak slowly :	Kulup lap
Where is the bridge :	Sampa ka-khà mo ?
To where does that road go :	P'idi lam di kà lo ?
Is the path difficult :	Lam-khà khákpo mo ?
It is an easy path to Namgà ?	Namgá na lam jam-tong du
How far is it from here to Tumlong ?	Nai-le Tumlong san-te t'à ring lü kà dzoi mo ?
How far is it from Darjiling to Sargong ?	Dorjeling-le Sargong lo t'à ring t'ung kà dzoi mo ?
Is it a long way to Làchhung :	Làchhung sante lam ring-kyam bo ?
Which is the way :	Di lam di kà mo ?
The village is near that monastery :	Audi chhoide di tsa-ne yul-ts'o dü
Do you know the way to go ?	Chhà-kyi gyu-she lam di she-sa
The path goes round the hill :	Lamkhà di gang kor kor ran chen du.
I am going to the Je-lep pass :	Ngarang Je-lep là lo gyu-do'in
It is a district full of ravines :	Yul rong-yul be
Where are you coming from :	Chhö kà-le yong do mo ?
Where are you going :	Chhö ka-khà na gyu do 'in

THE WEATHER.

The night is very dark :	P'iru di nyogi noksu be
Rain is going to fall :	Chhàb bàb she 'in
The rain will not cease to-day :	Chhàb di tàring mi chhé ong
I see the mist rising :	Nga humpo lang te tà
The ground is wet now :	Sà di tà-to bong-bo du'
The rain will soon come :	Di chhàb di gyoba ong she 'in
Can you run quickly :	Chhö gyoba chang ts'ug-ga (or chhug-ga)
The pass is filled with snow :	Là di kàng-ma chen kyang be
I am sinking in the snow :	Ngarang kàng nàngsha gu chen du'

When the rain ceases the air will grow clear :	Di chhàb di chhé-ne ngara salwa ong she du'
The sun is very hot :	Di nyim di nyogi t'um be
The sun will cause pain in your head :	Di nyim di chhö-kyi go nà-sha suk kya be
There is no moon to-night :	Tàring p'iru dou kan de me'
The wind is rising :	Lung di lang chen du'
Put wood on the fire :	Shing mi na t'suk
Shake the cloak well :	Chhàb-khebma zob-zob phyà
The wind is very cold :	Lung di nyogi khyàbo be
The air will be mild at Nar-ling :	Nga-ra di Narling za jampa ong she 'in

BUYING AND SELLING.

I want to buy some milk :	Nga um nyo go be
These Lepchas sell eggs :	Di Rong-pa di gongdo ts'ong
What will you sell me :	Chhö nga-lo kan ts'ong she bo ?
How much is the price of this :	Audi gong kà dzoi mo ?
What do you want :	Chhö kan go she bo ?
What have you got :	Chhö-lo kam bo ?
Nothing to-day :	Tàring kan de me'. (or) Tàring mipo :
I want nothing :	Mingo ("not wanted.")
Do you sell tea, butter, salt :	Chhö chà, mar, ts'à ts'ong bo ?
Can you get me any meat :	Chhö nga-lo sha t'up tsug-ga ?
You ask too much :	Chhö nyogi gong zhu do' in. (or) zhu chen du'.
Your price is very high :	Chhö-kyi rin di ma-nyung be.
I cannot give that price :	Nga gong di p'in mi ts'uk.
I will give you 10 rupees for that book :	Nga chhö lo tiruk chu tamba p'in yong audi chho di tanda lé.
I want twenty rupees for it : that is the exact price :	Nga di ten lé tiruk khe-chik go ; audi rin zhib-chha di be.
Go away : I don't want the thing :	Long song : Ngà-lo chhà-khà di mingo.
What have you got in that bag :	Chhö audi gyiup di nangsha kan ta bo ?
Show me some other things :	Nga-lo chhà-khà zhü-ma di ten nang.
I want to buy a knife :	Nga-lo ki-chhung chi nyo go.
That is not a good goat :	Audi ràma di lem min du'.
Give me two rupees for it :	Nga-lo tiruk nyi phintang di tenlé.
Have you any boots to sell :	Chhö ts'ong khen hlam du'bo ?
Give me another :	Zhü-ma nga-lo tong.
Are you a Wallung man or a Sikkim man :	Chhö Wallungki mi bo, ya-men ne Dai-jong ki mi bo ?
Come again to-morrow :	Nga-ro lok-te shok.
I want nothing to-day :	Nga tàring kan de mingo.

PREPARING AND EATING FOOD.

Make the water boil :	Chhu kol p'yà
Make the fire burn brightly :	Mi di leba bao zo'.
Bring the fish in a basket :	Nya di tséó ná-sha bak shok.
Bring the eggs : be careful :	Gongdo di bak shok : U'ip !
Bring some hot water now :	Ta-to chhu t'um chi bak nang.
Put tea in the tea-pot :	Chà-lo chàmbi ná-shá zhàk.
I do not want tea to-day :	Ngá táring chà mingo.
Will you eat tsampa in the tea :	Chhö tsampa chà ná-sha sà she bo?
Give me some bread : I don't want pak (sops) :	Ngá lo khu átsichi nang : nga pak mingo.
I shall dip bread in the meat-gravy.	Nga khu di shà-ruk ná-sha pák she 'in
Toast this meat at the fire :	Di shà di mī dün-tu sek p'yà.
Place the dishes on the table :	Pákna so-só di chen-t'e tengkha zhàk.
I shall eat rice this evening :	Ngá táring p'iru chum sà she 'in.
Have you any :	Chhö-lo átsichi bo?
Make the dumplings hot :	Shurbu di t'um p'yà.
I am eating dinner now ; go away :	Nga ta-to to (or *sama*) sà do 'in ; lok song !
She cannot eat rice :	Moi chum sà mi ts'uk be,
Shut your eyes ; open your mouth :	Chhö kyi mi-do tsum ; chhö-kyi kha gyang.
Give me the cup which is on the table :	Chen-t'e tengkhá karyo' di nga-lo nang tang.
Do you drink tea or beer :	Chhö chhang t'ung do bo, cha t'ung do bo?
Cover the ashes : bank up the fire (lit : " put the fire to bed.")	Mi-dak kàp ; mi nyál zhak.

HORSES AND GUNS.

Is this a quiet horse :	Ta audi nyambu bo?
Sir, it is :	Lha ; là-so. *(or)* Kusho, là du'.
Can it run quickly :	Di gyoba chang chhug-ga.
How-old is the horse :	Di tá di lo kà dzü som bo?
It is four years' old :	Di-lo lo zhi 'in.
Give the horse its food :	Ta-lo ri-kyi to tong.
Get bamboo leaves for the horse :	Nyuk kyi dámá t'ub tà di ten-le.
Make the horse ready :	Tà di t'al-tik p'yà.
Put on the saddle :	Tà-ga di zhak.
Have you the whip :	Chhö-lo buiko di yöp nya'.
Have you the whip : (less politely)	Chho-lo buiko di du bo?
Bring me a warm coat :	Nga-lo kolàk t'umpo chi bak shok !
Where is my gun :	Nge mindá ka-khà mo?

The gun-stock is dirty.	Gumda di malebo be.
Lengthen the stirrupstrap :	Yob-t'ak di ring-po p'yà.
Now, the other one :	Ta-to, zhü-ma-di.
Bring the powder : Be careful :	Médze bak shok. Riko gyimbo !
Can you shoot with a gun :	Chhö mindá kyap ts'ug-ga.
There are leopards in that hill :	P'idi gang di teng-kha sà t'ub be.
Come behind me; don't make a noise :	Nge so-le shok ; ur ma kyap !

SHOOTING IN THE HILLS.

See ! a leopard :	Tá ! sá chi.
It went behind that rock :	Tàk-kyi gyab lo song.
Go softly like a snake :	Byü dem jampo gyu !
Carefully ! Don't cough :	U'ip ! lo-cham ma kyap.
Stop ! Come back here :	Khok ! nái lók-te shok.
I have hit him :	Nga kho-lo dung chhé.
Give me the other gun :	Mindá zhü-ma nang.
Take care ! He is coming at us :	Riko gyimbo ! kho nga-chhok lo ong chen du'.
Beat that long grass :	Di tsà ring-po di dung.
Take your bamboo stick :	Ri-kyi pà-shing bák song.
We must climb up this hill :	Gang audi tengkha dzek go.
I am going down the kud :	Nga ghad teng-lo gyuchen du'.
Sit down ! Wait till I come :	Sà dü ! Nga ma ong sànte gü.
Wait here and watch :	Nái kug-te dü.
Yes, Sir, yes :	Kà-so, kàs.
I have seen some deer :	Nga khà-shà t'ong-chhé.
When ? Just now :	Nam bo ? Ta-to, ta-to.
Is the ground firm :	Sà di taktà bo ?
Do you see peacocks in this part :	Mábja di sà-chhà audi t'ong chen bo ?
What other birds are here :	P'yà zhü-ma nái kam bo ?
Go out of the way :	Lam-khá long song !

ENGAGING COOLIES.

I want twelve coolies (carriers) :	Nga-lo bák-khen chu-nyi go be.
You will need twenty for so much baggage :	Chhö-lo toi ma-nyung nyam-po khe-chik go she be.
How much will each coolie carry :	Bak-khen so-só kà dzü bak nang she bo ?
Thirty seers each coolie :	Bak-khen bak-khen sir sum-chu so-so.
How much will you give each man per day :	Mi so-só lo nyim di nyim di gong kà dzü p'in she bo ?
I will give wages and food :	Ngarang là to p'in she 'in.
I will give each man four annas a day :	Nga mi so-só lo nyimdi nyimdi anna zhi p'in she 'in.

The custom in Sikkim is five annas :	Shrol di Dai-p'ong-kyi anna ngá du'.
Your load is light :	Chhö kyi toi di yang-ke be.
This is not a heavy box :	Di dom di jhi-chen min du'.
Lift up the box :	Di dom di yà t'o.
Can this woman carry like a coolie :	Pum audi bak khen chi dem bak nang chhug-ga.
She can carry more than a man :	Mo mi chi lé chà-khà chhe bák nang chhuk.
Where is your tie-rope :	Chhö-kyi ri-yung di kà-khà mo.
Start now : make haste :	Tà-to gyuk : gyoba p'yà.
I shall want two mules :	Nga-lo te nyi go nyi 'in.
Wait at the bridge until I arrive :	Nga ma lep sán-te sampa di za gü.
Wait at the temple until you see me :	Chhö nga-lo ma t'ong sán-te gompa di za gü.
You are an idle man :	Chhö mi shailo (shé-lo) chi mé.
You sleep all day :	Chhö nyim-kyam nye bo é.
Lift up that basket on her back :	Tsé-o audi mo-i gyap kha yà t'o.
You are always sitting down :	Chhö àtong-màche sa dü chen be.

AT AN INN.

Where is the landlord :	Nā-bo di kà-na du'.
I am the landlady ; Sir Salaam :	Ngarang nā-mo yin, ku-sho, chhà' pe.
I want lodgings this night please :	Nga-lo nā-ts'ang tàring p'iru di go nyà.
Sir ; you are welcome :	Ku-sho ; chhà pe' zhu nyà.
Many thanks :	T'uk je chhe.
I am tired : please shew the bed :	Nga t'ang chhe po'in ; nye-sa di ten-nang.
Is there a bathing-tub :	Khyu-zong chi mo?
The bed is very hard :	Nye-sa di nyogi takta be.
The bed is not clean :	Nye-sa di tsang-mo min du'.
There is no other :	Zhü-ma chi min' du'.
There are lice—bugs—on it :	Di tengkha ō-chhō—deshi—du'.
Please shut the door :	Gom di tsum nang.
Shake the coverlet well :	Khebma zob-zob zhe !
Give me a light :	Nga-lo chū-mi p'in tang.
What is the charge :	Nà-là kà dzü mo?

TALK ON RELIGION.

There is only one God :	Di könchho di chik-po khar-kyang du'.
There is none besides the true God :	Könchho ngotok di man-na min du'.
Jesus Christ came down from Heaven :	Ye-shu Màshika nàm-kha le bap song.

He came into the world to speak tidings from God :	Kho jig-ten nà-sha ong zhe Könchho kyi lön ser-nyi.
Christ told men of another better world than this present one :	Mashika-kyī audi jigten di le jigten zhü-ma chi lem be lap song zhe.
When we die we shall enter a new life in Heaven :	Ngacha shi-ne ts'e sarpo chi namkha nà-sha t'ob nyi 'in.
We shall not enter another body in this world :	Ngacha pumpo zhü-ma nà-sha audi jigten di tengkha gyu ma ong.
We shall not be born again as animals or birds :	Ngacha semchen tarung p'yà lokte kye chung ma ong.
Jesus Christ died for you :	Ye-shu Màshika chhö kyi tandà le shi song.
He died to make payment for your sins :	Khorang, chhö-kyi kyön kyi rin p'in nang khen-kyi ten le, shi song.
I believe in Jesus Christ :	Ngarang Ye-shu Màshika lo yi chhe du' in.
Alas! you do not believe :	Ho-kye! chhö yi mi chhe-so.
Pray to God to shew you the real truth :	Könchho lo mönlàm kyap tàng chhö lo empa ngotok di tennyi.
Christ is the true thing and He died as substitute for all :	Màshika di nga-wo kho rang di be; kho yang mi t'am-che kyi ts'abpo shi song.
Buddha became a good man ; but he never obtained happiness.	Chomdende mi lem chi chung song; kalte na-mong gàmochen mi t'ob song.
You reach happiness when your sins have been forgiven :	Chhö-kyi dikpa di sal chung ne chhö-kyī gàmochen dub song.

THE LORD'S PRAYER IN DE-JONG KE.

Cho-wo yi Monlam.

Kye ngàchà-ki Yàb! Nyi-rang tà-to nàm-khà-i nà-shà du'. Chhö-kyi ming di dàmbu ser go. Chhö-kyi gyà-si p'eb she gong tang! Nàm-khà-i nà-shà chhö-kyi kù-gyur di dub-te, audi dem jigten tenkha nyen she go. Nge nyim-chen to-za di nga-lo nyim nyim p'in tang. Ngembu dàk lo nö kyal-khen mi zö-ne, audi dem nge dik-pa sal p'ya sol-lo! Nga-lo dikpai ts'ö zung khen di nà ma nàng. Onte ngempo le nga-lo tol nyà. Gyà-si, wangbu, ràkchen, kyang, nyi-rangchen be. Amén.

MISCELLANEOUS SENTENCES.

How far is it from here to the head of the pass :	Nài le làptse sàn-te t'à ring t'ung kà dzü mo?

What is the name of that peak?	Gang-tse p'idi kyi ming kà de'su?
What is the use of that flag?	Audi dar di kam p'yà du' mo.
That woman wears a long plait of hair:	Pum audi kyà hlow-wa chi kün chen du'.
What is the use of putting the shell on your hand:	Lak-koi tengkha t'ung di chhuk-te, p'ent'o kam bo?
Paint worn by Tibetan women on their cheeks:	Tüi-ja.
Shell worn on wrist:	T'ung-khà.
Long plait of hair worn:	Kyà hlow-wa.
Dandi bearer (of Darjiling):	Dandi bàk khen.
A China-man:	Gyà-nak-pa; or gyà-mi.
Cholera:	Nyà-lok.
Revenue Superintendents of the twelve districts into which Sikkim is divided.	Kà-zi (Bkà-gzigs).

GEOGRAPHICAL NAMES IN SIKKIM.

CHIEF TOWNS AND VILLAGES.

Tam-lóng (or Famous from Afar) the capital on the Labrong hill above the River Dig (Dig-chhu). Height above sea-level 5290 feet. Lat : 27°26′ N. Long : 88°38′ E.

Gàntak	Lingtam	Sung-ma	Ri-nog (Ri-ogtu)
Sinik	Namgá	Ràk-long	Gna-tong
Kartok	Tumtong	Dub-de	La-geb
Youngten	Dé-nga	Te-mi	Chungtong
Sangabang	Jhà-tang	Pemiong	Tungu
Seriong	Singtam	Brak (Ṭak)	Phà-lung
Sàmdong	Rupkam	Ter-wan	Mo-mé.

MONASTERIES (CHHOIDE AND GOMPA).

Lab-rong (Bslab-rong) the chief religious foundation in Sikkim where the chief lama of the country resides. His rank is that of a Khempo or abbot and he is popularly styled Kyap Gön Lama or the lama-protector. Tamlong is the lay-town of Lab-rong.

Pemiongchi	Ramt'ek
Ṭashiding	Lin-gye
Sangyechiling	Emchhi
Nobling	P'adre
Dalling	P'adung
Ralong	P'ensung
Rinchhenpong	De-tong
Kyets'operi	Gya-tong
Dubde	Rin-khim
Màli	Ling-t'em
Senang	Tà-lung
Yan-gong	Là-chhen
Ling-tse	Chung-tong
Namchi	Là-chung
Barmi	Sàm-dong
Gart'ok	

PRINCIPAL MOUNTAINS.

KANGCHHENJ'ENGA or Kangchhendzonga. The first name meaning "the five kings of the great snows" and the second name "the five treasure-boxes of the great snows." This mountain, commonly called Kinchinjunga by Englishmen, and Khambu Karma by the Sikkim Bhutias, has five summits, the two highest of which are 28,156 and 27,815 feet respectively. So extensive is the top of the mountain that these two peaks are in reality about 2 miles distant from each other.

KYAB-RU or the Horn of Protection. Is situated S. E. of the above on the Nipalese frontier of Sikkim. Alt. 24,030 ft. 5 miles S. E. is another peak of same name.

KYOKCHIRANGKANG (The Snows of the Secret king or The Snows of the Crooked Head). A peak between Kyabru No. 1 and Kyabru No. 2 sometimes reckoned with these two and one more to the west as forming the 4 peaks of one grand summit. Alt. 22,450 ft.

P'OHUNRI or, more probably, P'o-yum-ri which would mean Father and Mother Mountain. On the eastern frontier of Sikkim; about 6 miles from the Donkya Pass, but separated from the pass by a deep valley. Alt. 23190 ft.

KANGCHENJHO (The Lord of the Glaciers) some 20 miles inward from the northernmost frontier line. Alt. 22550 ft.

JHOM-YUMO (The Queen of Dwarfs) on the northern frontier line in Long. 88° 34' E. Notwithstanding its name has a height of 22,290 ft.

YAK-CHAM (The Lover of Good) or Lama A-den (the Lama-fashioned) sometimes known in Reports as "D. No. 3." Alt. 19,202 ft.

PANDIM, possibly Pàndem (Dpà ldem) or Statue of Bravery. Is a lofty peak south from Kangchhenjenga and east of Kyabru; and in the view from Darjiling seen slightly to the right of the former mountain. Alt. 22,020 ft. Distance from Darjiling, 36 miles.

SI-YIMBO WANGCHIM; alt. 22,300 ft. and SI-NYOLCHUM; alt. 22,570 ft. are, in the view from Darjiling, the two summits nearest to Pàndem on the right hand side. Glancing to the right from that mountain they appear in the order in which we have named them.

NAR-SENG (Uplifted as a Nose) the nearest to Darjiling of the really lofty summits. Only 32 miles distant. Alt. 19,150 ft.

There are, in addition to the above, numerous snowy peaks on the Sikkim-Tibetan border line, stretching N. N. E. of Kanchhenjenga all of which attain an altitude higher than 22,000 ft. One, due north of the famous mountain and only 20 miles distant from it, reaches nearly to 25,000 ft. The view of this lofty peak from Darjiling is completely blocked out by the interposition of Kangchhenjenga. The name of the stupendous mountain thus hidden has not yet been clearly ascertained from the natives; nor yet those of at least twelve others in close proximity to it.

PRINCIPAL RIVERS (CHHU).

TEESTA.—This is only the Gurkha name of the RANG-NYO as it is called by the people of Sikkim.

RANG-NYIT, not the "Rungit" or "Rungeet" as commonly termed. There are two rivers of this name :—Rang-nyit Chhem-po chhu (great Rang-nyit River) rising in the centre of Dé-jong amid the heights of Mount Mà-long (alt. 14,500 ft.) and flowing due south until British territory is reached, when it makes a sharp turn to the east and, after a course of some 12 miles as the southern boundary of Independent Sikkim, flows into the Rang-nyo (Teesta) at Pà-shok. (2) Rang-nyit chhung chhu (Little Rang-nyit river) now lying wholly within British territory. Rises in Mount Tonglu and flowing to the north of Birch hill empties itself after a tortuous course into the greater Rangnyit at Sing-la t'om.

RAMMAM rises in the Singilela range and flowing east along the southern boundary line of Sikkim joins the Great Rang-nyit at the sharp bend of the latter eastward.

RANG-BI rises in the Gamot'àng lake district near Kang La and the Tangkün Pass, 20 miles due south of Kangchhenjenga.

LA-CHHUNG rises in the lofty heights stretching between Kangchhenjho and the Don-kya Pass. It is a big river and after a long southerly course joins the TA-LUNG Chhu (which arrives from the regions of Kangchhenjenga) at the Ling-t'em Monastery. The combined rivers thence flow due south under the new name of the Rang-nyo or TEESTA. The latter river, we know, eventually flows into the Brahmaputra at a point near the Garo hills.

MILITARY TERMS AND TITLES.

The ruler of Sikkim depends for military defence on Tibet; and the people of Tibet depend on China *(Mahátsin)*. The Senior Ampàn, one of the two representatives of the Emperor of China at Lhàsà, is the Director General of the military affairs of Tibet and Sikkim. Nominally he only *advises* the native Tibetan Privy Council at Lhàsà. In reality it is he who, under cover of the Council, exercises complete control over both the Chinese and the Tibetan soldiers in the country. The ordinary army numbers 6500, out of which under ordinary circumstances 500 only are Chinese, the remainder Tibetan. Of the 6000

Tibetan troops, 3000 are relegated into a reserve force on half-pay and are permitted to engage in agricultural pursuits, being called out for exercise at strictly regular intervals. These latter are styled *yul-mák* or "country-force." The *yul-mák* on the peace footing are subject to the Dzong-pön (jong-pön) of the particular Dzong or fortress to which they belong. Under the Ampàn is a *Mák-pön* or professional military comptroller of the whole army. The whole army comprises 6 regiments; and from the *Mák-pön* the official rank in each regiment descends as follows :—

Dá-pön = General (commanding 1 regiment of 960 men divided into two battalions or *ru-ná.*)

Ru-pön = Colonel (over battalion of 480 of above men.) — *Ru-pön* = Colonel (over battalion of 480 of above men.)

Gyá-pön = Major (over 240 of above.) — *Gyá-pön* = Major (over 240 of above.) — *Gyá-pön* = Major (over 240 of above.) — *Gyá-pön* = Major (over 240 of above.)

Four *Ding-pön* = Captain; each over a *ding-ts'o* or company of 60 men. — 4 *Ding-pön* = Captain; each over a *ding-ts'o* or company of 60 men. — 4 *Ding-pön* = Captain ; each over a *ding-ts'o* or company of 60 men. — 4 *Ding-pön* = Captain ; each over a *ding-ts'o* or company of 60 men.

Under the *Ding-pön* are *Chu-pön*, a sort of corporal, one to every 10 men.

Mák-mi a soldier
Mák-pung army
Mák-ts'o regiment
Ru-ná battalion
Ding-ts'o company
Mák-t'ab war
Kyá-pung the enemy
T'áb-mo an engagement
Pung-nön re-inforcements
Mák-ts'o nön-ma ditto

T'áb-rú earthworks, intrenchments.
Mák t'áb-she to fight.
Kyáp-lok p'yá-she to retreat.
Ts'ámpur or *gyok* a cannon.
Mindá a rifle.
Kyap-she to fire.
Kyáp-du' yin are firing.
Kyáp-she 'in will fire.
Gyá mi ts'o Chinese.
P'ö-kyi mi ts'o Tibetans.